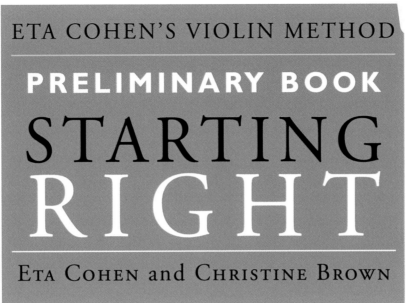

ETA COHEN'S VIOLIN METHOD

PRELIMINARY BOOK

STARTING RIGHT

Eta Cohen and Christine Brown

ILLUSTRATIONS BY HEATHER ANDREWS

A separate part giving accompaniments for
piano or second violin is included

NOVELLO

EXCLUSIVELY DISTRIBUTED BY

HAL•LEONARD®

INDEX OF PIECES

Cover design by Miranda Harvey

FOREWORD

Starting Right is intended for complete beginners who have no previous knowledge of notation and is based on the golden rule of "teach only one point at a time". If this rule is followed, the pupil is hardly aware that he or she is advancing and there will be no tears at any stage!

Rhythm

Rhythm exercises are introduced before any pitch notation and a rhythm exercise should be practised before each new point of rhythm is introduced in a piece. This prepares the pupil for the melodies which follow. Only crotchets, minims, dotted minims and their respective rests are introduced, as quavers would require quicker placing of the fingers than is desirable at this stage.

Notation

Many teachers advocate the aural approach rather than the visual. Our experience is that if the two are developed together as in *Starting Right* the difficulties of reading are almost non-existent and the pupil starts from the beginning to associate the *look* of a note with its *sound.* This provides the best foundation for aural perception, visual memory and sight reading.

Another method often used is to teach the pupil to play all the open strings first, gradually adding all the fingers. This usually produces bowing and reading difficulties and it delays the study of attractive tunes which the children are able to sing before playing. The tunes in the second half of *Starting Right* are all within the compass of the scale of D and therefore are easy to read, sing and play.

Fingering

In order to lead up to these pieces gradually, the pupil first learns open string D and adds only one note at a time until the D scale is completed. The difficulties of reading are then minimal, as the notes of the D scale are the easiest because there are no leger-lines to read. The tunes are well within a child's vocal range and as words are included even the simplest melodies become interesting and aural training is developed together with visual training.

It is suggested that all the tunes in this book are first played pizzicato in banjo position, thus lessening the strain of the difficult under-chin position.

When the pupil has become accustomed to handling the instrument he/she can play pizzicato under chin. Later, this is followed by bowing which should first be studied in the *Eta Cohen Violin Method* Book I, starting at Step 6. Here the "one point at a time" approach is used.

Again the advantages of D and A string playing are evident. On these strings the height of the bowing arm is quite natural and a good sound is most easily achieved. This contrasts with the often unpleasant sounds produced when playing on the G and E strings.

One final bonus about using only the middle strings is that the difficulty of tuning is minimised.

Accompaniments

Piano accompaniments are provided for 28 pieces while ten have parts for a second violin. Where no piano is available the teacher may play the right hand of the piano part on the violin, except in the 'concert' items, numbers 27, 28, 33, 37, 42 and 45.

There are no dynamics in the accompaniments because the young violinists will not be ready to make any variation of tone, but the pianist should try to capture the mood of each piece.

Eta Cohen
Christine Brown

CONTENTS

CLAPPING DUETS

Clap each part, then try clapping as a duet with your teacher.

TICK-TOCK

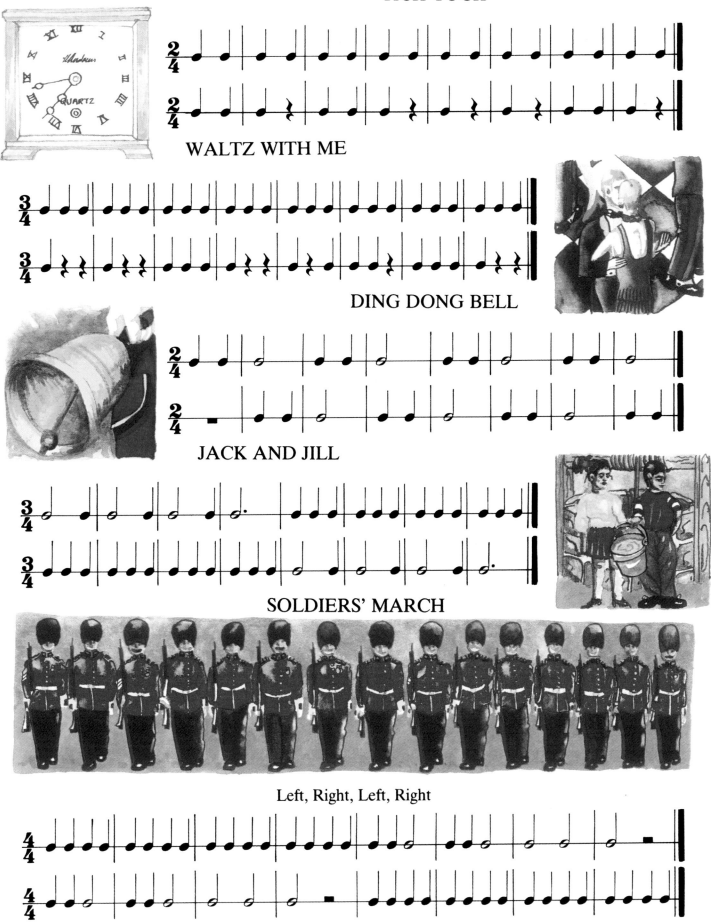

WALTZ WITH ME

DING DONG BELL

JACK AND JILL

SOLDIERS' MARCH

Left, Right, Left, Right

The note **D** on the D String

Clap both parts of TICK-TOCK and WALTZ
WITH ME (on page 1) before you play these pieces

1

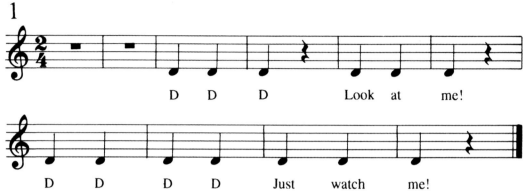

D   D   D   Look   at   me!

D   D   D   D   Just   watch   me!

2

D   D   This   is   D

Play   this   lit – tle   tune   for   me.

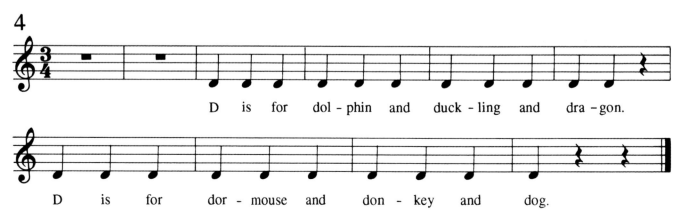

3

D   D   What   is   for   tea?

Fish   fin – gers,   jel – ly   and   cus – tard   for   me.

4

D   is   for   dol – phin   and   duck – ling   and   dra – gon.

D   is   for   dor – mouse   and   don – key   and   dog.

VIOLIN DUETS

Clap both parts of DING DONG BELL and JACK AND JILL
(on page 1) before you play the pupil's part of these pieces.

BELLS OF AMSTERDAM

4

The notes **D** and **E** on the D string
Open string and first finger

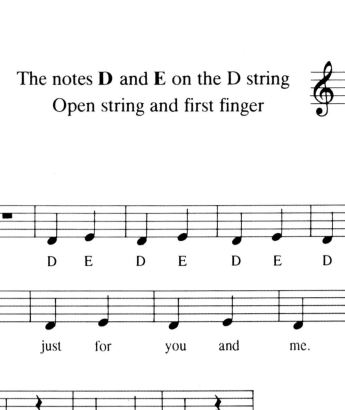

8

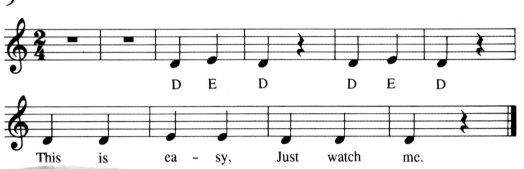

D E D E D E D

Play this just for you and me.

9

D E D D E D

This is ea – sy, Just watch me.

10

Off we go, quick and slow,

We can play both high and low.

11

Skip – ping and danc – ing and sing – ing a song,

Skip – ping and sing – ing and danc – ing a – long.

Write in the names of these notes

<u>D</u>   <u>E</u>   __   __   __   __   __   __

The notes **D, E** and **F sharp**
Open string, first and second fingers

12   THE HILL

Up   we   climb,   down   we   run,

up   we   go,   we   have   such   fun.

13   THE SPINNING WHEEL

Round and   round the   wheel goes   spin - ning

round   and   round   and   round   it   spins.

14   THE KITTEN

Lit - tle   kit - ten   small   and   white,

can   you   stay   with   me   to - night?

15   SQUIRRELS

Squir - rels   are   red,   squir - rels   are   grey.

We   love   to   find   them   and   watch   them   at   play.

Write these notes as crotchets

D   E   F sharp   F sharp   E   D   F sharp   E   D

6

The notes **D, E, F sharp** and **G**
Open string, first, second and
third fingers on the D string

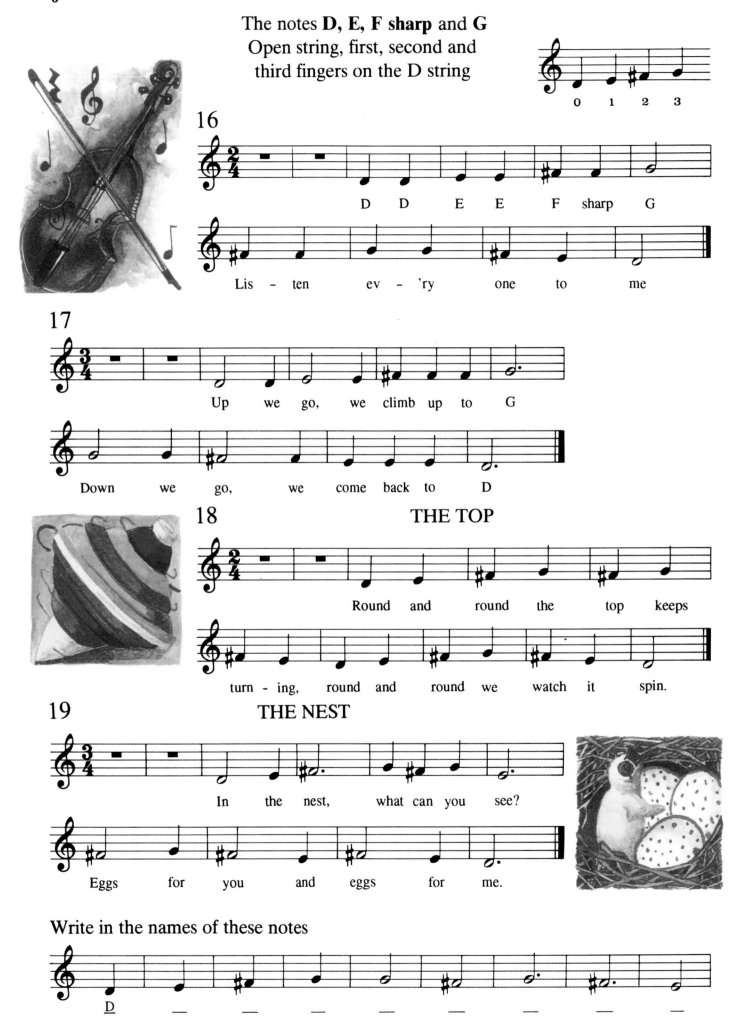

16

D   D   E   E   F sharp G

Lis - ten   ev - 'ry   one   to   me

17

Up   we   go,   we   climb up to   G

Down   we   go,   we   come back to   D

18   THE TOP

Round   and   round   the   top   keeps

turn - ing,   round   and   round   we   watch   it   spin.

19   THE NEST

In   the   nest,   what can you   see?

Eggs   for   you   and   eggs   for   me.

Write in the names of these notes

D   __   __   __   __   __   __   __

LOOK AT ME!

2 THIS IS D

© Copyright 1991 Novello & Company Limited Cat. No. 91 6176

3   **WHAT IS FOR TEA?**

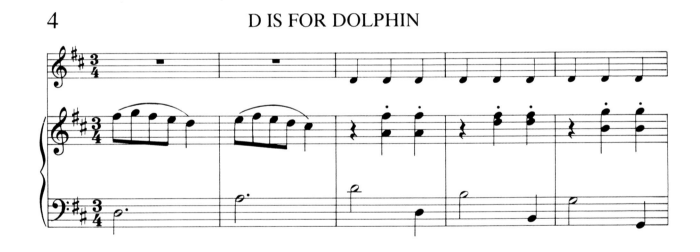

4   **D IS FOR DOLPHIN**

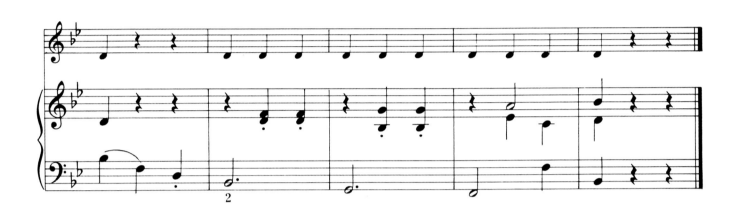

8 D – E – D – E

9 THIS IS EASY!

10   OFF WE GO

11   SKIPPING AND DANCING

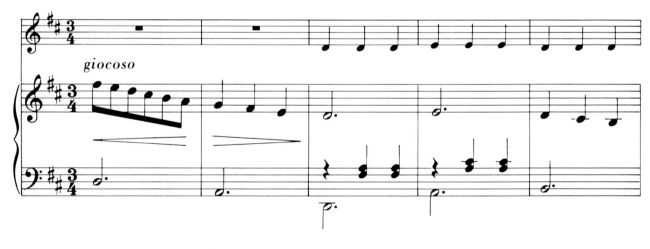

12 THE HILL

13 THE SPINNING WHEEL

14

THE KITTEN

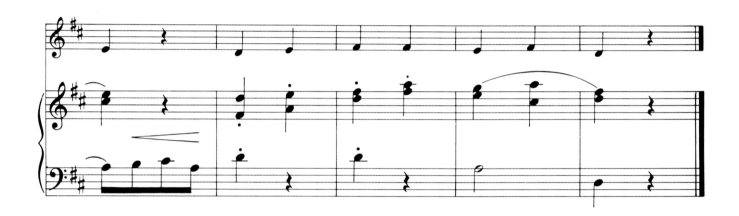

15

SQUIRRELS

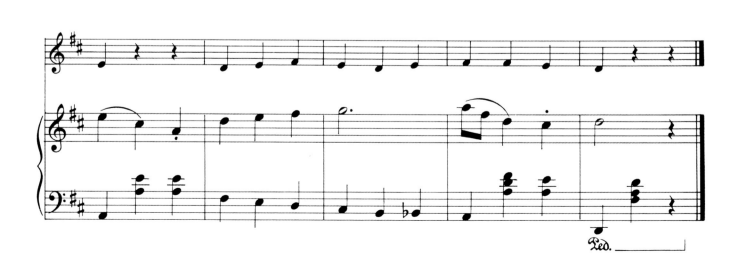

16
D – D – E – E – F sharp – G

17
UP WE GO

18 THE TOP

19 THE NEST

20   PEASE PUDDING HOT

21   WELSH FOLK SONG

10

22   FRENCH DANCE 'Les Bouffons'   ARBEAU

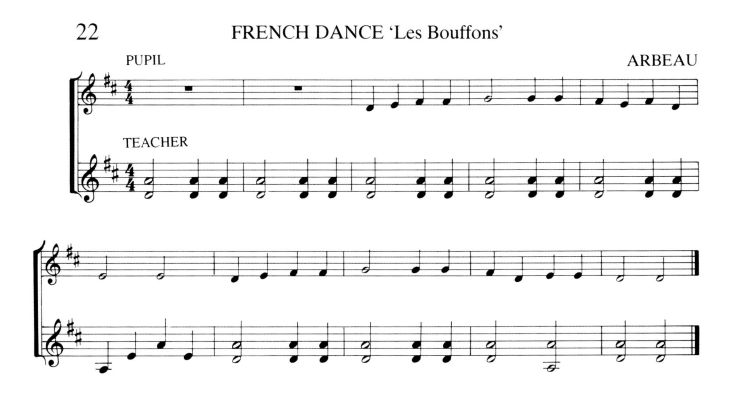

23   FRENCH LULLABY 'Dodo l'enfant do'

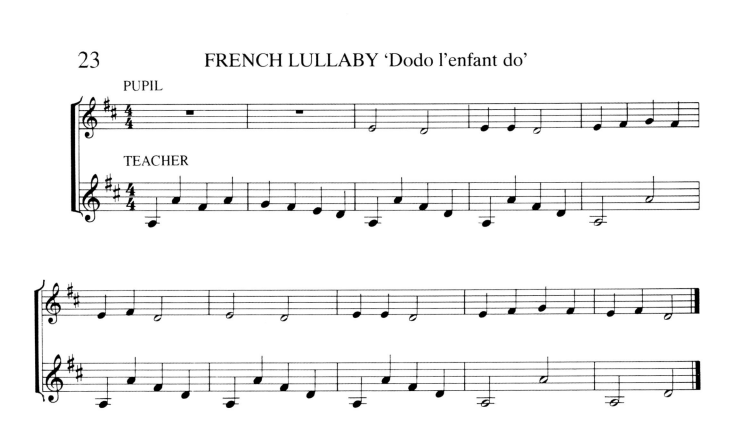

24 A – A – A

25 WHAT CAN I PLAY?

26 HANSEL AND GRETEL

27 IRISH LULLABY

28 JINGLE BELLS

31   A – B – A

32   ANGELA'S SKIPPING

33 LULLABY

36   FRENCH SONG 'Savez-vous planter les choux?'

37   MEDIAEVAL MELODY

GUILLAUME d'AMIENS

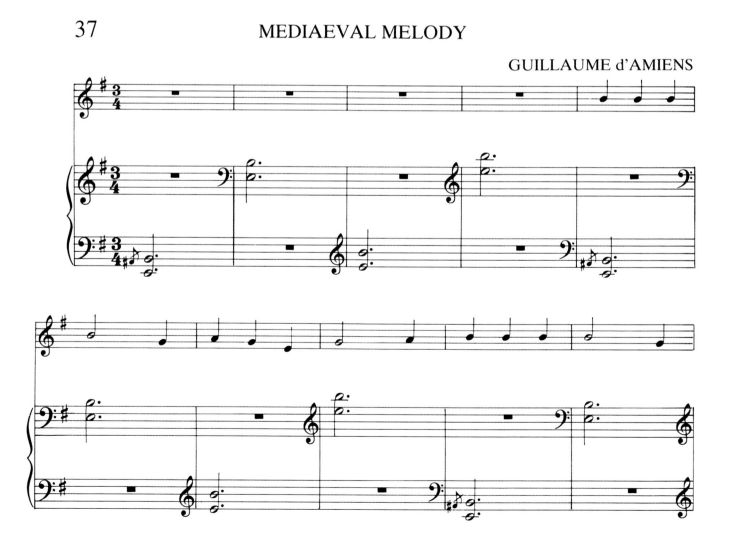

38   A — B — C sharp — D

39 DAFFODILS

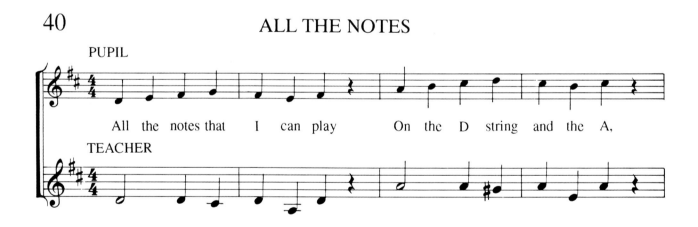

40 ALL THE NOTES

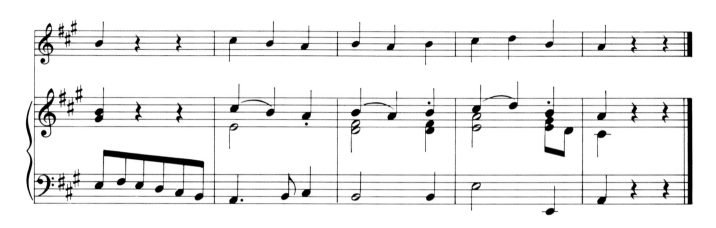

PUPIL

All the notes that I can play On the D string and the A,

TEACHER

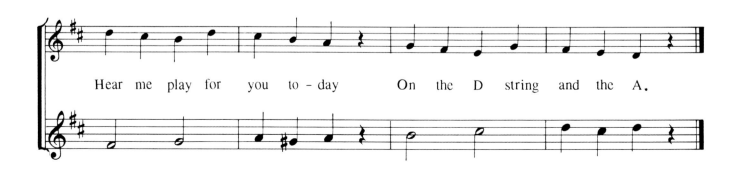

Hear me play for you to-day On the D string and the A.

42 LI'L LIZA JANE

45 HICKORY, DICKORY, DOCK

Tunes on **D, E, F sharp** and **G**
Clap SOLDIERS' MARCH (on page 1)
before you play these pieces

20 PEASE PUDDING HOT

Pease pud-ding hot, Pease pud-ding cold.

Pease pud-ding in the pot, Nine days old.

21 WELSH FOLK SONG

Sum - mer's past, Now at last,

Leaves must fall, Gol - den brown.

© Copyright Oxford University Press 1974. Reproduced by permission.

22 FRENCH DANCE 'Les Bouffons'

ARBEAU

23 FRENCH LULLABY
'Dodo l'enfant do'

Write these notes as minims

E D F sharp G E F sharp G E D

8

The note **A** on the A string

24

A A A I can play.

Is my A in tune to - day?

25

A A What can I play?

I can play A for you, This is the A.

26 HANSEL AND GRETEL

27 IRISH LULLABY

28 JINGLE BELLS

29 BYE, BABY BUNTING

30 GOOD KING WENCESLAS

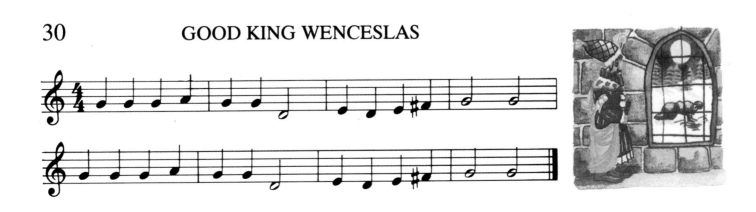

The notes **A** and **B** on the A string
Open string and first finger

31

A B A A B A

This is how I like to play.

32

An - ge - la's skip-ping a - long the green lane.

Dav - id is dream-ing he's driv - ing a train.

33   LULLABY

1 2 3 4 Sleep my sweet,

Slum - ber deep. Mo - ther's watch - ing near you.

Sleep my sweet, Slum ber deep,

Rest soft - ly 'til morn - ing

Write in the names of these notes

A — — — — — — — —

34 WESTMINSTER CHIMES

35 BOYS AND GIRLS

Boys and girls come out to play, The
moon is shin - ing as bright as day.
Leave your sup - per and leave your sleep And
join your play - fel - lows in the street.

36 FRENCH SONG
'Savez-vous planter les choux?'

Sa - vez-vous plan - ter les choux à la mo - de,
à la mo-de? Sa-vez-vous plan-ter les choux à la mo-de de chez nous?

37 MEDIAEVAL MELODY

GUILLAUME d'AMIENS

1   2   3   4

Write these notes as dotted minims

B   A   G   F sharp   E   D   F sharp   A   B

The notes **A, B, C sharp** and **D**
Open string, first, second and
third fingers on the A string

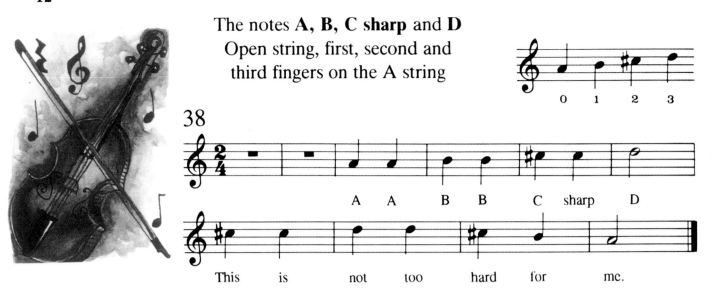

38

A A B B C sharp D

This is not too hard for me.

39 DAFFODILS

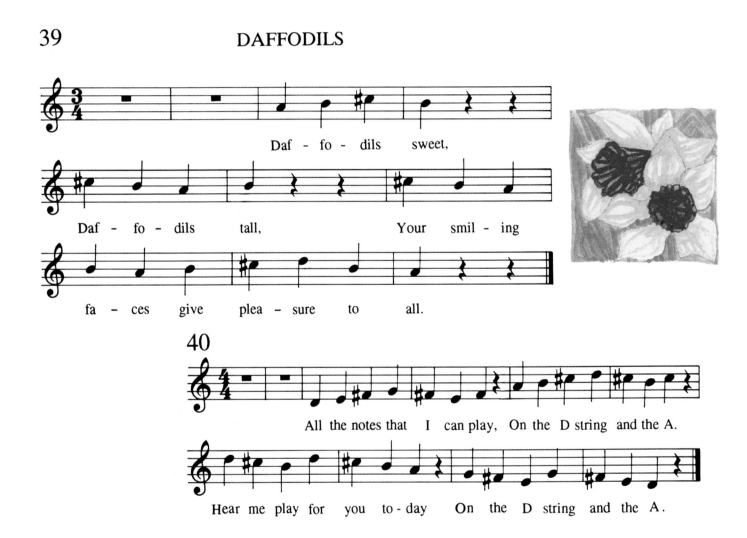

Daf – fo – dils sweet,

Daf – fo – dils tall, Your smil – ing

fa – ces give plea – sure to all.

40

All the notes that I can play, On the D string and the A.

Hear me play for you to - day On the D string and the A.

Write in the names of these notes

C sharp ___ _ _ _ _ _ _ _

From now on key-signatures will be used.

41   **COCK ROBIN**
Suffolk Folk Song

42   **LI'L LIZA JANE**

43   **THE FOUR LOVES**

The Hart he loves the high wood, The Hare he loves the hill, The Knight he loves his bright sword, The La-dy loves her will.

14

44   FROM HEAVENS HIGH

45   HICKORY, DICKORY, DOCK

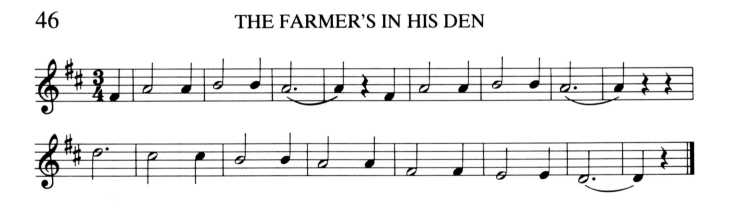

46   THE FARMER'S IN HIS DEN

47   St. PAUL'S STEEPLE

48   **GOODBYE**

Up in the air, sail - ing on high,

Ted - dy is wav - ing, wav - ing good - bye.

Printed in the EU - 10/15(195440)

ETA COHEN'S
VIOLIN METHOD

This highly respected violin course is the first choice for teachers in the UK and abroad. It includes the following material:

STARTING RIGHT

Covers the vital preliminaries to playing for the young beginner violinist, enlivened with colour illustrations. Includes accompaniment parts for violin duet and piano. (NOV916176)

BOOK 1

Student's Book (NOV916136) Violin part with teacher's notes. Divided into 30 Steps, each introducing a new technical point.
Accompaniment Book (NOV916137) Contains the piano accompaniments.
Teacher's Book (NOV916175) Violin duet parts and notes.
Learning to Play the Violin Three cassettes (NOV916167-01/02/03) and an instruction book (NOV916167) designed to accompany Book 1. The recordings provide the piano accompaniments and second violin parts.

BOOK 2

Student's Book (NOV916170) Every exercise and piece in this book is designed to improve and introduce new aspects of technique.
Accompaniment Book (NOV916171) Violin duet part and piano accompaniment.

BOOK 3

Student's Book (NOV916172) 30 graded lessons introducing technical points gradually, supported by numerous pieces.
Accompaniment Book (NOV916173) Contains the piano accompaniments.
Teacher's Book (NOV916174) Violin duet part.

BOOK 4

Complete Book (NOV916177) A wealth of valuable repertoire and studies which develop vital new areas of study. Includes violin part and piano accompaniments.

YOUNG RECITAL PIECES

Supplementary material for the Method books 1-4: three books of enjoyable pieces for young violinists, including many well-known works in easy arrangements. Each book contains the violin part and piano accompaniment.

Book 1 (NOV916180)
Book 2 (NOV916181)
Book 3 (NOV916182)

EASY VIOLIN DUETS

Ideal for group teaching, introducing ensemble playing and making the early stages of learning more fun. These duets are carefully graded to be used alongside Starting Right and the Method books.

Book 1 (NOV916184)
Book 2 (NOV916185)
Book 3 (NOV916186)